¡Mole!

Rio Nuevo Publishers®
P.O. Box 5250, Tucson, Arizona 85703-0250
(520) 623-9558, www.rionuevo.com

Text and photography © 2006 by Rio Nuevo Publishers.

All photos by W. Ross Humphreys, except pages 51, 77 by Robin Stancliff
(food styling by Tracy Vega; thanks to Connie Choza for the beautiful
setting). Thanks to Iliana de la Vega for allowing photos to be taken in her
cooking classes in Oaxaca, Mexico, and to Feliza Méndez Gutiérrez
for preparing mole by hand in the tradition of her family in her home
in San Martín Tilcajete, Ocotlán, Oaxaca, Mexico (page 52).

Library of Congress Cataloging-in-Publication Data

Doland, Gwyneth.
¡Mole! / Gwyneth Doland.
     p. cm. — (Cook west series)
Includes index.
ISBN-13: 978-1-887896-86-3
ISBN-10: 1-887896-86-4
1. Mexican American cookery. 2. Sauces. I. Title.
TX715.2.S69D65 2006
641.5'972—dc22

                    2006020402

Design: Karen Schober,
Seattle, Washington.

Printed in Korea.
10 9 8 7 6 5 4 3 2 1

¡Mole!

GWYNETH DOLAND

COOK WEST SERIES

contents

xxxxxx

introduction

What is mole? Many of us have become enamored of this complex, intoxicating dish, but relatively few of us know what's in it (besides chocolate) or how it's made. Mole's most famous ingredient—chocolate—is actually a minor player in a sauce that can have more than two dozen ingredients, including tomatoes, raisins, sesame seeds, whole cloves, and oregano. Many moles don't contain any chocolate at all!

The Spanish word *mole* (pronounced MOE-lay or MOE-leh) comes from the Aztec word *molli,* which was used by the pre-Columbian indigenous peoples of Mexico to refer to the sauces they made by pounding dried chiles with seeds and nuts in giant mortars. The Spaniards brought to the New World many ingredients, especially spices, which were incorporated into the native sauces.

Today, mole remains the most beloved dish of Mexico, and a different version is made by nearly every cook. But several stand out as traditional favorites. The famous *mole poblano* is named for the Mexican state of Puebla, where it is reported to have been made for the first time by a pious nun in the late seventeenth century. A thick, rich, and complex sauce made with several kinds of chiles, it is one of the few moles that actually does call for chocolate.

Despite the popularity of Puebla's mole, the Mexican state of Oaxaca is the heart of mole country. Oaxaca is known for its seven moles—an incredible variety that ranges from the deep smokiness of *mole chichilo* (often made as a stew) and *mole negro* to the surprising fruitiness of *mole manchaman-teles*, the fresh herb flavors of *mole verde*, the subtle variations of red chiles in *mole colorado* and *mole coloradito*, and the bright, light *mole amarillo*. In Oaxaca, street vendors sell heaps of mole pastes and spice mixtures, but some cooks still make their own, grinding the chiles and spices by hand on a coarse stone metate. Others outsource the work, taking their ingredients to be ground at a local mill.

Cooks in other parts of the country make their own moles, too, using different kinds of chiles or adding more nuts or different fruits to create infinite variations. And that's the beauty of mole. This is not one recipe with a strict list of ingredients. No, the mole family is a group of elaborate and time-consuming dishes that range from thick sauces to not-so-thick soups. There are no hard and fast rules about what's called a mole and what's not. The primary ingredients—especially the chiles—and the basic techniques are important, but pretty much everything else is up to you, what's in your kitchen, and what's in the market.

One thing nearly all moles have in common is effort. Mole is never simple; it is at its best when it is most complex, most time-consuming. Because of the long list of ingredients and many steps involved in the preparation of a mole, the dish is most often made for special occasions. In Mexico it is served at Christmas, Day of the Dead celebrations, weddings, and funerals, and on patron saints' days. I think you'll find that making mole makes the occasion.

TECHNIQUE

The technique for making mole is complex but boils down to this: poach a chicken or a turkey. Then toast some dried chiles, nuts, and spices on a cast-iron skillet. Soak the chiles in the stock, then grind them up with the nuts and spices. Cook some tomatoes, tomatillos, onions, garlic, and a few other fruits and/or vegetables, then puree them. Mix the chile puree and the vegetable puree and fry it all in oil. If you're using chocolate, stir it in, then add the poached meat and simmer. That's it! You're ready to go!

Of course it is more complex than that, but once you get the hang of it, you'll find you don't need a recipe at all. All you need are the right ingredients and the right equipment. The good news is that once you've made a batch of mole, you can do a million things with it. The mole can become a sauce for enchiladas, a filling for tamales, a thickening additive to other soups, or a flavor boost for barbecue sauce. The possibilities are endless.

INGREDIENTS

Chiles Chiles provide the structure and primary flavor for mole, providing not just heat, but fruity, smoky, sweet flavors. In Oaxaca, the many varieties of locally grown chiles give their moles a flavor impossible to reproduce. Luckily, these chiles are becoming more and more available, especially from Internet retailers (see Sources, page 86).

ANCHOS are dried poblano chiles. They are broad-shouldered, with a dark red color and mild, raisiny flavor. They are used in mole coloradito, mole rojo, mole manchamanteles, and mole poblano.

CHILHUACLES are hard to find in the U.S., although they are much prized in Mexico. About the size of a small ancho, these chiles come in amarillo, rojo, and negro (or yellow, red, and black) forms. The fresh chilhuacle amarillo has a tart, slightly bitter flavor that makes it a popular ingredient in mole amarillo. The dried chilhuacle rojo is dark red, with a medium, sweet heat and raisiny, figgy flavor. It is used in mole coloradito and mole rojo. The dried chilhuacle negro is expensive, but sought after for the deep, rich flavor with hints of dried plum and licorice. It has a subtle but lingering heat and is used for mole negro.

CHIPOTLE CHILES are smoked chiles, most often smoked jalapeños. These small dried chiles have an intense smoky flavor and sharp heat. They are available dried or, more commonly, canned in tomato-based adobo sauce.

COSTEÑOS AMARILLOS are short, skinny chiles with a light citrus flavor that makes them the fresh chile of choice for mole amarillo. They are very hard to find in the U.S.

GUAJILLOS are bright red chiles that resemble dried red New Mexico chiles, but their skins are far tougher, and they must be soaked in hot water longer before they soften. They are quite hot, but very flavorful; used in mole negro, mole coloradito, mole amarillo, and mole manchamanteles.

GÜERO CHILES, pale yellow fresh chiles with a spicy kick, have become more common lately in grocery stores. If you find them, use them for mole amarillo.

JALAPEÑOS are short, dark green, and very hot fresh chiles, with a bright, tart flavor. They are used in mole verde.

MULATO CHILES, a type of dried poblano, are very dark with a smoky, raisiny flavor; used for mole negro and mole poblano.

NEW MEXICO DRIED RED CHILES are big, long, skinny red chiles. Thin-skinned with a bright, fruity flavor, they are some of the most common red chiles in grocery stores.

PASILLAS are long, skinny, dark brown chiles with a medium-hot kick and a rich, complex flavor. They are also sometimes called chiles negros. When fresh, they are called chilacas. They are used in many moles, including mole negro, mole rojo, mole chichilo, and mole poblano.

POBLANOS, the fresh form of anchos, are heart-shaped, dark green chiles with a mild heat. They are used for mole verde.

SERRANOS, native to the mountains north of Puebla, Mexico, are small, dark green chiles that look like skinny jalapeños. Like jalapeños, they are quite hot with a fresh, citrusy flavor.

Herbs and Spices These flavorings play an important role in mole, adding layers of complexity. Some are relatively easy to find, some nearly impossible. Leaving one out will not ruin your mole, but adding them will add a great amount of flavor. The cheapest way to buy spices is in bulk, either at your natural foods store or online (see Sources, page 86).

ALLSPICE tastes like a combination of cinnamon, nutmeg, and cloves—hence the name. Look for whole berries.

AVOCADO LEAVES. Many recipes call for this hard-to-find ingredient. Some cooks suggest substituting a small amount of anise seed to hint at the leaves' flavor.

CANELA, also known as Mexican cinnamon or Ceylon cinnamon, is different from the tropical evergreen bark that Americans are used to, which is known as cassia cinnamon. Canela is much thinner-skinned, mild, and sweet. Once you taste it, you won't want to substitute the thick, harsh cassia cinnamon (nor will you want to submit your blender to it).

CLOVES. Use whole cloves if you can. The flavor is much better.

CUMIN SEEDS, toasted and ground, are far superior to ground cumin.

EPAZOTE is a strong-tasting fresh herb that some people love and some hate. It is commonly found dried in Mexican markets because it is always used when cooking beans (it is believed to reduce gas). There is no substitute.

HOJA SANTA is the large leaf of a plant native to Mexico. Its "herby" flavor is hard to describe. It has no substitute.

MEXICAN OREGANO (*Lippia graveolens*) has a stronger flavor than Mediterranean oregano. If you use Mediterranean oregano in your mole sauce, you'll think it tastes like spaghetti sauce. Don't do it. Look for Mexican oregano in the spice aisle or in the Mexican foods section of your grocery store.

Nuts and Seeds Most moles contain nuts and seeds. Almonds, peanuts, pecans, pumpkin seeds, and sesame seeds are often used in combination to give this sauce body and richness. If you want to experiment, consider using hazelnuts, cashews, or other nuts.

Fruits and Vegetables Tomatoes, tart green tomatillos, onions, garlic, raisins, plantains, pineapple, apple, prickly pear cactus paddles, and squash are all common mole ingredients, although it's doubtful you'd find them used all together.

Chocolate   Mole's most famous ingredient is not used in every mole, although it is a vital ingredient in mole poblano. Remember that even when mole contains chocolate, the resulting sauce never tastes like ice-cream topping. Chocolate merely plays well with the other ingredients, adding depth, some fat, and a little silkiness to the texture.

In Mexico there are still cooks who grind—by hand!—their own cacao beans for mole, but most people use store-bought chocolate. Especially popular, and surprisingly common in the U.S., is Mexican drinking chocolate, such as Ibarra, that's flavored with sugar, cinnamon, and almond.

EQUIPMENT

If you don't have a stone metate for grinding, how will you ever make mole? These few pieces of equipment will help you greatly.

BLENDER.   As most American kitchens don't have stone metates for grinding chiles, spices, and chocolate, we must rely on the clumsy, too-powerful work of the blender to do our grinding. Note: a food processor is no match for the blender.

CAST-IRON SKILLET.   A large, cast-iron skillet, which becomes nonstick with use and age, is very useful for toasting spices, heating tortillas, and frying meats. They are inexpensive, so do yourself a favor and get one before attempting a mole.

COMAL.   A comal is a flat cast-iron griddle, used for toasting chiles and cooking tortillas. You can use a regular cast-iron skillet instead, but you might find you need two at once.

DOUBLE BOILER.   Cooking delicate foods such as chocolate requires gentle methods, like using a double boiler. Instead of cooking (and probably burning) the chocolate over direct heat, it is put in a bowl or other pan set over a pot of boiling water. The steam cooks the chocolate safely.

DUTCH OVEN. A deep cast-iron or enameled cast-iron Dutch oven will regulate heat well for frying and simmering a big batch of mole.

SIEVE. You'll need to press all sorts of purees through a sieve, and no other piece of kitchen equipment can substitute. Luckily they are inexpensive.

SPICE GRINDER. I use a small coffee mill to grind small amounts of spices. Use a separate one for coffee, or your canela will taste like espresso.

Mole Rojo

xxxxx

Makes about 5 cups

**4 cups turkey
or chicken stock**

**2 dried ancho chiles,
stemmed and seeded (see
Sources, page 86)**

**2 dried guajillo chiles,
stemmed and seeded (see
Sources, page 86)**

**2 dried mild New Mexico red
chiles, stemmed and seeded
(see Sources, page 86)**

$1/_4$ cup slivered almonds

$1/_4$ cup chopped pecans

**3-inch piece of canela (see
Sources, page 86)**

4 whole cloves

4 allspice berries

**1 small onion,
roughly chopped**

2 cloves garlic

**1 large tomato,
roughly chopped**

**1 cup sweetened
dried cranberries**

**2 tablespoons lard
or vegetable oil**

**2 ounces bittersweet
chocolate, broken into bits**

Salt

Dried cranberries are not traditionally included in mole rojo, one of the lighter moles, but I think the bright, concentrated flavor of the fruit fits perfectly in this brilliant red sauce. If you like, you can make a more traditional mole rojo with $1/_4$ cup red raisins instead of the dried cranberries. If you have chilhuacles rojos, use them in place of some of the anchos, guajillos, or New Mexico red chiles. Otherwise, this blend works well. You can simmer poached poultry in the sauce for the last 20 minutes of the cooking time, or use this as a sauce for enchiladas or huevos rancheros.

In a saucepan over high heat, bring the stock to a boil.

In a cast-iron skillet over medium heat, toast the chiles on both sides until they soften slightly and become aromatic. Transfer to a medium-sized, heat-safe bowl and add enough hot stock to cover. Keep the chiles submerged with a small plate or saucer.

In the same skillet, toast the almonds, pecans, canela, cloves, and allspice berries until the almonds brown slightly and both nuts start to release their aroma. Transfer the nuts and spices to the blender.

Add the onion and garlic to the dry skillet and cook until the onions char a little and the garlic gathers some golden patches. Add the tomato and cranberries and cook until the tomato releases its juices and then thickens, about 15 minutes. Transfer the mixture to the blender.

Using a slotted spoon, transfer the chiles to the blender and puree, adding enough stock to make a thick sauce. Press the mixture through a fine-meshed sieve set over a large bowl.

Add the lard or vegetable oil to a large, heavy-bottomed saucepan or Dutch oven set over medium heat. Fry the mole for 2 minutes, stirring constantly, then add the chocolate and remaining stock and simmer 20 minutes. Season to taste with salt and serve.

Mole Verde

xxxxxx

This green mole is made with pepitas (roasted and hulled pumpkin seeds—look for them in the bulk aisle of your natural foods store). Versatile mole verde tastes great over chicken, pork, fish, and even steak.

Put the tomatillos and stock in a medium saucepan, bring to a boil, reduce heat, and simmer 15 minutes.

Meanwhile, in a cast-iron skillet over medium heat, toast the pepitas, cumin seeds, cloves, and canela until the seeds start to pop and turn golden. Transfer the seeds and spices to the pitcher of your blender and puree with about 1 cup of the stock from the tomatillo pot. With a rubber spatula, scrape the puree into a small bowl and set aside.

When the tomatillos are done, transfer them to the empty blender. Add the jalapeño and poblano chiles, onion, and garlic, and puree, adding a little stock if necessary. Scrape this puree into a large bowl.

Makes about 3 cups

3/4 **pound tomatillos, husked and washed**

3 **cups chicken stock**

1 **cup pepitas**

1/4 **teaspoon cumin seeds**

4 **whole cloves**

3-**inch piece of canela (see Sources, page 86)**

2 **jalapeño chiles, stemmed, seeded, and chopped**

1 **poblano chile, stemmed, seeded, and roughly chopped**

1/2 **medium onion, roughly chopped**

2 **cloves garlic**

1 **tablespoon vegetable oil**

1 **cup cilantro leaves, washed and dried**

3 **romaine lettuce leaves, washed and dried**

In the same skillet over medium heat, fry the pumpkin seed mixture in the oil until it browns slightly.

Meanwhile, add the cilantro and lettuce leaves to the blender and puree with 1 cup of the stock. Add the pureed leaves and the tomatillo mixture to the skillet and heat through. Serve immediately.

Mole Coloradito

xxxxxx

Makes 6 cups

4 cups chicken or beef stock

6 dried ancho chiles, stemmed and seeded

6 dried New Mexico red chiles, stemmed and seeded

1/2 cup sesame seeds

4 black peppercorns

3-inch piece of canela (see Sources, page 86)

6 allspice berries

1/3 cup raisins

1 medium onion, quartered

6 cloves garlic

1 pound ripe tomatoes, cored and chopped

1 tablespoon Mexican oregano (see Sources, page 86)

2 tablespoons vegetable oil

New Mexico's red chile sauces are kin to the red moles of Mexico, and cooks in both places use red chile sauces with beef and chicken, especially for enchiladas and tamales. This recipe uses New Mexico red chile pods instead of guajillos because they are sweet, fruity, and easy to find. You can also use guajillos or chilhuacles rojos if you have them. You'll find another version of Mole Coloradito from Oaxacan chef Iliana de la Vega on page 57.

In a saucepan over high heat, bring the stock to a boil.

In a cast-iron skillet over medium heat, toast the chiles on both sides until they soften slightly and become aromatic. Transfer to a medium-sized, heat-safe bowl and add enough hot stock to cover. Keep the chiles submerged with a small plate or saucer.

In the same skillet, toast the sesame seeds, peppercorns, canela, allspice berries, and raisins until the seeds turn pale gold and the raisins plump slightly. Transfer the seeds and spices to the blender.

Add the onion and garlic to the dry skillet and cook until the onions char a little and the garlic gathers some golden patches. Transfer the onions and garlic to the blender.

Add the tomatoes and Mexican oregano to the skillet and cook 15–20 minutes. The tomatoes will soften, release their juices, and then thicken.

When the tomatoes are cooked, transfer them to the blender. Remove the chiles from the soaking broth and add them to the blender. Puree with 2–3 cups of the broth, enough to make a thick sauce.

In a heavy-bottomed saucepan or Dutch oven, heat the vegetable oil over medium-high heat. Add the pureed sauce and fry 3 minutes, then reduce the heat and simmer 30 minutes.

Mole Negro

xxxxxx

The defining characteristic of this mole—its deep, dark color—is achieved by blackening the seeds of chilhuacles negros, pasillas negros, and other dark chiles. If choking on the fumes of burning chile seeds is your idea of a good time, then be sure to blacken them on your stovetop with all of the windows closed up tight. The rest of you would be well advised to blacken the chile seeds outside on your grill. Simmer poached poultry in the sauce for the last 20 minutes of the cooking time, or use the sauce for roasted or grilled meats.

Preheat the grill to high. In a cast-iron skillet set on the grate, cook the reserved chile seeds until blackened. (You'll want to stand upwind of the grill.)

Back inside, bring the stock to boil in a saucepan over high heat.

In a cast-iron skillet over medium heat, toast the chiles on both sides until they soften slightly and become aromatic. Transfer the chiles to a medium-sized, heat-safe bowl and add enough hot stock to cover. Keep the chiles submerged with a small plate or saucer.

In the same skillet, toast the sesame seeds, almonds, canela, and cloves until the nuts are golden and the spices become aromatic. Transfer the seeds, nuts, and spices to the blender.

Add the onion and garlic to the dry skillet and cook until the onions char a little and the garlic gathers some golden patches. Add the tomato and dried plums and cook until the tomatoes

Makes about 4 cups

6 dried chilhuacle negro (or mulato) chiles, stemmed and seeded, seeds reserved

6 dried pasillas negros, stemmed and seeded, seeds reserved

6 dried guajillo chiles, stemmed and seeded, seeds reserved

4 cups chicken stock

$1/4$ cup sesame seeds

$1/2$ cup slivered almonds

2-inch piece of canela (see Sources, page 86)

4 whole cloves

2 tablespoons lard or vegetable oil

6 cloves garlic

1 small white onion, peeled and roughly chopped

1 large tomato, roughly chopped

$1/2$ cup dried plums, pitted

1 dinner-roll-sized bolillo, piece of challa, or brioche, torn into pieces

2 ounces bittersweet chocolate, chopped

Salt and brown sugar

release their juices and thicken. Transfer the mixture to the blender.

Add the bread, soaked chiles, and about ¼ cup of the blackened chile seeds to the blender and puree, adding enough stock to make a thick, smooth sauce.

In a large, heavy-bottomed saucepan or Dutch oven over medium heat, melt the remaining 2 tablespoons of lard or oil. Add the pureed sauce and fry about 3 minutes, stirring constantly. Add the chocolate, stirring until melted; reduce heat and simmer, about 20 minutes. Season to taste with salt and brown sugar.

Nancy's Mole Poblano

xxxxxx

Makes about 6 cups

4 dried ancho chiles, stemmed and seeded

8 dried red New Mexico chiles, stemmed and seeded

2 chipotle chiles in adobo

2 cups chopped onion

4 cloves garlic, minced

4 medium tomatoes, chopped

¹/₄ cup sesame seeds, divided

(ingredients continue on next page)

This streamlined recipe comes from my friend and colleague Nancy Gerlach. It is adapted from the version that appears in The Spicy Food Lover's Bible, *a book she wrote with Dave DeWitt, who is affectionately known as "The Pope of Peppers." Mole poblano comes from the Mexican state of Puebla (hence the name poblano), but as the most famous and most beloved dish in Mexico, it is served nearly everywhere. There are many stories about its creation, but most of them give credit to a seventeenth-century nun, Sor Andrea, who invented the dish in the kitchen of the convent of Santa Cruz. This mole is usually served with poached turkey, which is simmered in the sauce for the last 30 minutes of the cooking time.*

In a cast-iron skillet over medium heat, toast the ancho and New Mexico chiles on both sides until they soften slightly and become aromatic. Transfer the chiles to a medium-sized, heat-safe bowl and pour in enough hot water to cover. Keep the chiles submerged with a small plate or saucer for 15 minutes. Drain the chiles and discard the water.

Put the rehydrated ancho and New Mexico chiles, chipotles, onion, garlic, tomatoes, 2 tablespoons of the sesame seeds, almonds, tortilla, raisins, cloves, cinnamon, and coriander in your blender. Puree the mixture and, with the motor running, add enough stock to form a smooth sauce. (You may have to do this in batches.)

Heat a large, heavy-bottomed saucepan or Dutch oven over medium heat, add the lard or oil, and, when it is hot, add the chile puree and simmer for 10 minutes, stirring frequently. Add more broth to the sauce to keep it smooth, and to thin if it gets too thick. Reduce heat, stir in the chocolate, and cook over very low heat for 30 minutes or until the sauce has thickened. Season to taste with salt and pepper. Serve garnished with the remaining 2 tablespoons of sesame seeds.

1 cup toasted almonds, chopped

$1/2$ corn tortilla, torn into pieces

$1/2$ cup raisins

$1/2$ teaspoon ground cloves

$1/4$ teaspoon ground cinnamon

$1/4$ teaspoon ground coriander

4–6 cups chicken or turkey stock

3 tablespoons lard or vegetable oil

2 ounces bitter chocolate

Salt and freshly ground pepper

Mole Manchamanteles

xxxxxx

Serves 8

6 cups chicken stock

4 dried ancho chiles, stemmed and seeded

4 dried guajillo chiles, stemmed and seeded

6 whole cloves

3-inch piece of canela (see Sources, page 86)

1/2 cup slivered almonds

6 cloves garlic

1 small onion, roughly chopped

1 pound tomatoes, roughly chopped

1 tablespoon vegetable oil

2 ripe plantains, peeled and diced into 1/2-inch cubes

2 cups diced pineapple (1/2-inch cubes)

1 1/2 pounds chicken and/or pork, diced into 1/2-inch cubes

2 cups water

2 tablespoons brown sugar

One of the seven moles of Oaxaca, manchamanteles is unusual because it usually includes pineapple, plantain, and other fruits. The name translates as "tablecloth-stainer" because of the way the chunky sauce seems to get all over the place as you're eating it. For a milder sauce, use mild New Mexico red chiles in place of the guajillos.

In a saucepan over high heat, bring the stock to a boil.

In a cast-iron skillet over medium heat, toast the chiles on both sides until they soften slightly and become aromatic. Transfer the chiles to a medium-sized, heat-safe bowl and add enough hot stock to cover. Keep the chiles submerged with a small plate or saucer.

In the same skillet, toast the cloves, canela, and almonds to the skillet until the nuts are golden and the spices become aromatic. Transfer the spices and nuts to the blender.

Add the garlic and onion to the skillet and cook until the onions char a little and the garlic gathers some golden patches. Add the tomatoes, reduce heat and simmer 15–20 minutes, or until tomatoes are softened and thickened.

Meanwhile, add the chiles and their soaking stock to the blender and puree. (Depending on the capacity of your blender, you may need to do this in batches.) Press the mixture through a sieve.

Heat the vegetable oil in a large, heavy-bottomed saucepan or Dutch oven over medium-high heat. Fry the pureed mixture for 2–3 minutes. Add the plantains, pineapple, meat, and water. Bring the mole to a boil, reduce heat, and simmer 20 minutes, or until meat is cooked through. Sweeten to taste with brown sugar. Serve immediately or store in the refrigerator. This mole stores and reheats well.

Mole Chichilo Stew

xxxxxx

Many moles are actually made as stews, and this is the least well-known and most unusual of the Oaxacan moles. As in the mole negro, the chile seeds are burnt to add color and flavor, but for mole chichilo, corn tortillas are also charred. The result is a distinctive, smoky flavor. This recipe is adapted from one I found in Zarela Martínez's book, The Food and Life of Oaxaca. *If you like, you can also add masa dumplings (recipe follows) for the last 5–10 minutes of the cooking time.*

In a large stockpot, place 2 of the garlic cloves, the onion, beef, pork, salt, and 8 of the peppercorns. Add enough water to cover and bring to a boil. Reduce heat and simmer over low heat, partially covered, for 15 minutes. Using a slotted spoon, remove the meat to a bowl. Continue simmering the stock for 15 more minutes. Strain the stock through a sieve, rinse out the stockpot, and return the strained stock to it. Bring the stock to a boil, then reduce heat and simmer, gently.

Meanwhile, in a cast-iron skillet over medium heat, toast the chiles on both sides until they soften slightly and become aromatic. Transfer the chiles to a medium-sized saucepan. Char

Serves 6–8

6 unpeeled cloves garlic, divided

1 unpeeled medium onion, quartered

2 pounds beef stew meat, cut into 1 1/2 -inch cubes

2 pounds pork butt or shoulder, cut into 1 1/2 -inch cubes

1 teaspoon salt

12 peppercorns, divided

4 dried guajillo chiles, stemmed and seeded

6 dried chilhuacle rojo chiles (or ancho chiles), stemmed and seeded

3 corn tortillas

10 dried avocado leaves (see Sources, page 86)

4 whole cloves

1 tablespoon dried Mexican oregano (see Sources, page 86)

1/2 cup masa harina (see Sources, page 86)

the tortillas over an open flame (a stove-top burner, gas broiler, or outdoor grill) until completely blackened. Add the tortillas to the chiles and add enough water to cover by 3 inches. Bring to a boil, reduce heat, and simmer over medium-low heat for 10 minutes. Remove from the heat, drain, and transfer chile and tortilla solids to the pitcher of your blender.

In the same skillet, over medium heat, toast the avocado leaves for a few seconds on each side, until they become aromatic and slightly browned. Transfer 6 of the leaves to the blender and reserve the rest.

Add the remaining 4 peppercorns, cloves, Mexican oregano, and the remaining 4 garlic cloves to the blender, and puree with 1 cup of the reserved stock. Press the puree through a sieve over the simmering stock. Add the 4 remaining avocado leaves and season to taste with salt.

In a mixing bowl, combine the masa harina with about 2 cups water. Whisk the mixture into the simmering stock, adding it a little at a time, and continue to whisk until the stock thickens.

Add the reserved cubes of meat and simmer for 30 minutes or until the meat is tender. Serve in deep soup bowls.

MASA DUMPLINGS

In a large bowl, sift together the masa harina and salt. Pour the warm water over the sifted mixture and stir with a fork. Add the lard and, using your hands, work the mixture into a smooth dough.

To form the dumplings, take a small lump of dough and roll it into a ball about 1 inch in diameter. Holding the ball in the palm of one hand, use the thumb of your other hand to make a deep dimple in the ball. Repeat for the remaining dumplings. Let them rest 1 hour, covered with a damp dish towel, before adding to the stew.

Makes about 2 dozen

1 cup masa harina (see Sources, page 86)

1 teaspoon salt

$1/2$ cup warm water

1 tablespoon lard, cut into small pieces

Saffron-Scented Mole Amarillo

xxxxxx

This smooth mole gets its deep golden color from the combination of tomatillos, guajillo chiles, and delicate saffron threads. (Resist the temptation to use Mexican saffron, called azafrán, which comes from the safflower plant. It doesn't taste at all like real saffron, although it provides a similar color.) You can serve this versatile mole over any meat, tamales, or fish, or mix it with meat for an empanada filling.

In a saucepan over high heat, bring the stock to a boil.

In a cast-iron skillet over medium heat, toast the chiles on both sides until they soften slightly and become aromatic. Transfer the chiles to a medium-sized, heat-safe bowl, add the saffron threads, and pour in enough hot stock to cover. Keep the chiles submerged with a small plate or saucer.

Makes 4 cups

4 cups chicken stock

6 dried guajillo chiles, stemmed and seeded

$1/2$ teaspoon saffron threads

2-inch piece of canela

4 whole cloves

$1/3$ cup slivered almonds

$1/2$ teaspoon cumin seed

2 tablespoons lard or vegetable oil

1 medium white onion, diced

6 cloves garlic

1 pound tomatillos, husked, washed, and quartered

$1/3$ cup masa harina (optional; see Sources, page 86)

In the same skillet, toast the canela, cloves, almonds, and cumin seed until the nuts are golden and the spices become aromatic. Transfer the spices and nuts to your blender.

Add the onion and garlic to the dry skillet and cook until the onions char a little and the garlic gathers some golden patches. Add the tomatillos, stir to combine, and simmer, covered, until the tomatillos are cooked through, about 20 minutes.

Add the tomatillo mixture, chiles, and their soaking water to the blender and puree completely. Press the mixture through a sieve set over a large bowl.

Add the lard or oil to a large, heavy-bottomed saucepan over medium heat. Fry the mole for 2 minutes, stirring constantly, then add the remaining stock and simmer 20 minutes.

For a thin mole, serve as is; for a thick mole, mix ⅓ cup masa harina with water to form a smooth paste. Add it to the mole and cook 5 minutes, whisking constantly.

Mild and Chunky Mole Amarillo

xxxxxx

Makes about 4 cups

1 pound small yellow chiles

2 yellow or orange bell peppers

2-inch piece of canela (see Sources, page 86)

4 black peppercorns

4 whole cloves

1/3 cup white sesame seeds

2 tablespoons vegetable oil

1 onion, peeled and coarsely chopped

2 cloves garlic

6 tomatillos, husked, washed, and quartered

1 cup seafood or chicken stock

1 tablespoon honey

Kosher salt

This relatively easy mole has a sweet, mild flavor. I was inspired to make this when I found a profusion of small yellow chiles on sale at my local Mexican market. Chilhuacles amarillos are traditional but very rare, so use whatever kind of yellow chiles you can get your hands on and supplement with yellow bell peppers for color and sweetness.

Over the flame of your gas grill, stovetop, or broiler, blacken the skins of the chiles and bell peppers. Place in a large bowl and cover with plastic wrap for 15 minutes to loosen the skins. Remove the blackened skin from each chile and bell pepper by gently brushing with your flattened palm. Rinse your hand often in cool running water. Coarsely chop the chiles and bell peppers.

In a large cast-iron pan over medium heat, toast the canela, peppercorns, cloves, and sesame seeds for a few minutes until they're lightly toasted and aromatic. Transfer them to the blender. Sauté the onion and garlic until the onions soften. Add the chopped peppers and tomatillos, stir, and cook, covered, until the tomatillos are cooked through, about 20 minutes. Add the pepper mixture and stock to the blender and puree completely.

Add the oil to a large, heavy-bottomed saucepan or Dutch oven over medium heat. Stir in the honey and fry the mole for 5 minutes, stirring often. Add kosher salt to taste. Use immediately or store in the refrigerator for up to 3 days.

Orange-Honey Mole with Roast Duck

xxxxxx

Orange is not a traditional mole ingredient, but it is a traditional accompaniment to duck in other cuisines. This recipe calls for roasting a whole duck; you may also buy duck parts and roast them, although you won't be able to use the giblets to flavor the stock. Pull any extra meat from the carcass to use for Shredded Duck Quesadillas (see page 43). Serve with plenty of warm corn tortillas. A couple of other recipes in this book suggest or call for the Orange-Honey Mole sauce you will have left over after making this dish.

Preheat oven to 350 degrees F.

Remove the giblets from the duck cavity. Rinse the duck under running water, inside and out, and pat dry with paper towels. Prick the skin all over with a fork or the tip of a paring knife (don't pierce the meat). Sprinkle salt and pepper all over the duck and put it on a rack in a roasting pan, breast-side down. Roast about 40 minutes. Flip the bird so that the breast is facing up, and continue roasting another 40 minutes or until the inside of the thigh reaches 160 degrees F.

Once the duck is in the oven, put the giblets in a stockpot with the stock or water and oregano. Bring to a boil, reduce heat, and simmer while you make the sauce.

In a cast-iron skillet over medium heat, toast the chiles on both sides until they soften slightly and become aromatic. Transfer to a medium-sized, heat-safe bowl and add enough hot stock to cover. Keep the chiles submerged with a small plate or saucer.

Serves 4

1 duck, fresh or thawed (about 6 pounds)

Salt and freshly ground pepper

4 cups water or chicken stock

2 tablespoons Mexican oregano (see Sources, page 86)

3 dried ancho chiles, stemmed and seeded (see Sources, page 86)

4 dried pasilla chiles, stemmed and seeded (see Sources, page 86)

$3/4$ cup slivered almonds

$1/2$ cup golden raisins

2-inch piece of canela (see Sources, page 86)

6 whole cloves

1 tablespoon vegetable oil

$1/2$ medium onion

2 cloves garlic

3 Roma tomatoes, chopped

$1/4$ cup frozen orange juice concentrate

$1/4$ cup honey

2 tablespoons reserved duck fat or vegetable oil

2 ounces unsweetened baking chocolate, broken into small pieces

In the same cast-iron skillet, toast the almonds, raisins, canela, and cloves until the almonds are golden and the raisins puff slightly. Transfer this mixture to your blender.

Add the onion and garlic to the dry skillet and cook until the onions char a little and the garlic gathers some golden patches. Add the tomatoes and reduce heat. Cook until the tomatoes release their juices, then thicken, about 15 minutes. Add them to the blender.

With a slotted spoon, remove the chiles from the soaking stock and add them to the blender. Add the soaking stock, orange juice concentrate, and honey, and puree on the highest setting.

The duck should be just about done. If it is, take a ladle and scoop about 2 tablespoons of fat from the bottom of the pan. Place the fat in a large, heavy-bottomed saucepan or Dutch oven over medium heat. Carefully pour the contents of the blender into the saucepan. Stir well. Add the chocolate and stir until it is completely melted. Season with salt or add more stock, if necessary.

When the duck is cooked, remove it from the oven and allow it to cool enough to handle. Cut off the legs and carefully remove the breast meat. Remove the skin and fat from the breasts. Put the legs and breasts in the pot with the mole and simmer 20 minutes. Serve immediately.

Apple Butter Mole

xxxxxx

This dish was inspired by David Garrido and Robb Walsh's recipe for grilled pork chops in apple butter mole, which appears in their book Nuevo Tex-Mex. *Garrido and Walsh serve the sauce over grilled pork chops, and indeed it is delicious served over any grilled meat, but I like it even better when made with pork tenderloins that are cooked right in the sauce. This mole is also used in the Mashed Plantain Fritters recipe (see page 46).*

In a cast-iron skillet over medium heat, fry the onion, garlic, and chiles in 2 tablespoons of the bacon grease or oil. When the onions have softened, add the apple butter, chicken stock, cinnamon, and cloves. Bring the mixture to a boil, stirring, then remove from the heat.

Transfer the mixture to your blender and puree until smooth. Season to taste with salt and pepper.

Add the remaining lard or oil to a saucepan or skillet set over medium heat. Add the pureed mole and bring it to a boil, stirring constantly. Immediately reduce the heat and simmer the mole for about 20 minutes. Serve hot.

Makes about 4 cups

1/2 onion, roughly chopped

1 clove garlic, chopped

2 guajillo, pasilla, or New Mexico red chiles, stemmed and seeded

1 dried chipotle chile (optional)

4 tablespoons bacon grease or vegetable oil, divided

2 cups apple butter

2 cups chicken stock

1 pinch ground cinnamon

1 pinch ground cloves

Salt and freshly ground pepper

PORK TENDERLOINS IN APPLE BUTTER MOLE

In a skillet, melt the bacon grease or oil over high heat. Quickly sear the pork tenderloin pieces on all sides. Reduce heat, add about 4 cups of Apple Butter Mole, and simmer 20 minutes, or until the pork is just cooked through. Serve.

Serves 4

2 tablespoons bacon grease or oil

2 pounds pork tenderloin, cut into 4 equal pieces

White Chocolate Mole

xxxxx

Makes about 1½ cups

½ cup unsalted peanuts

¼ cup slivered almonds

¼ cup walnuts

2-inch piece of canela, broken into pieces

2 whole cloves

2 cups chicken stock

1 fresh poblano chile, seeded and chopped

2 fresh serrano chiles, seeded and chopped

1 small clove garlic

½ white Spanish onion, cut into chunks

5 animal crackers

½ stick (4 tablespoons) unsalted butter

½ cup chopped white chocolate

½ teaspoon salt

⅛ teaspoon freshly ground white pepper

This is my version of a recipe that Judy Walker, who is now food editor for the New Orleans Times-Picayune, *collected back when she worked at the* Arizona Republic. *Believe it or not, animal crackers are a common thickener for mole in Mexico, where the crackers are lighter and less sweet than their American counterparts. Serve this sauce over poached chicken breasts or fish.*

In a cast-iron skillet over medium heat, toast the peanuts, almonds, walnuts, canela, and cloves until the nuts are slightly golden and fragrant.

Transfer the nuts and spices to the pitcher of your blender, add the stock, and puree. Press the mixture through a sieve set over a bowl.

Put the strained nut mixture back in the blender with the chiles, garlic, onion, and animal crackers. Puree until smooth, then press through a sieve again.

In a large saucepan set over medium heat, melt the butter. Add the strained mixture to the pan and simmer, uncovered, until it thickens, about 15 minutes. If you're making the sauce ahead, remove it from the heat, cover, and refrigerate for up to a week. When you're ready to serve it, proceed to the next step.

Over low heat, add the white chocolate, stirring until it is completely melted and incorporated. Season to taste with salt and pepper and use immediately.

Morning-After Chilaquiles

xxxxxx

Serves 2

2 tablespoons vegetable oil

6 corn tortillas, sliced into
$1/2$-inch-wide strips

2 large eggs

1 cup Mild and Chunky Mole
Amarillo (see page 32)

1 jalapeño, stemmed,
seeded, and chopped
(optional)

$1/4$ cup chopped cilantro

This hearty breakfast will fortify you after a late night. In place of Mild and Chunky Mole Amarillo, you could substitute another cold or room-temperature mole, but a freshly made salsa would probably work better.

Pour vegetable oil into a large skillet over medium-high heat. Fry the tortilla strips in the hot oil until crispy; drain on paper towels.

Fry the eggs sunny-side up in the oil that remains in the skillet.

Distribute the tortilla strips evenly between two plates, top with eggs, mole, jalapeño, and cilantro, and serve.

Huevos Rancheros

xxxxxx

Eggs fried sunny-side up or over easy will spill their warm, rich yolks into the mole, which is what makes this dish so good. Use any leftover red or yellow mole.

In a small saucepan over low heat, gently warm the mole. If necessary, add enough water to reach the consistency of a thin cream soup.

Add 1 teaspoon of the bacon grease to a cast-iron skillet over medium-low heat. Fry 1 tortilla on each side until warmed and softened. Transfer the tortilla to a plate. Repeat with the remaining grease and tortillas.

In the same skillet, fry the eggs, seasoning with salt and pepper.

On one serving plate, pour a dollop of the mole and top with a prepared tortilla. Pour more mole over it, top with another tortilla, and pour more mole over that, spreading it over the surface of the tortilla. Top with the fried eggs, garnish with onion and cheese, and serve immediately.

Serves 2

1 cup Mole Rojo
(see page 16)

4 teaspoons bacon grease or unsalted butter, divided

4 corn tortillas

2 eggs

Salt and freshly ground pepper

$1/2$ small onion, chopped

$1/2$ cup shredded asadero cheese (see Sources, page 86)

Huevos Manchamanteles

xxxxxx

Serves 2

1 cup Mole Manchamanteles
(without meat, if possible)
(see page 26)

4 teaspoons bacon grease or
unsalted butter, divided

4 corn tortillas

2 eggs

Salt and freshly
ground black pepper

$1/2$ cup green peas

$1/2$ cup diced ham

$1/2$ cup crumbled
queso fresco

2 cups refried black beans
(optional)

2 cups fried plantains
(optional)

This is a play on the Yucatecan dish huevos motuleños, a relative of the more familiar huevos rancheros. In the Yucatan, these eggs are topped with a spicy salsa and served with refried black beans and fried plantains. For this recipe, I've substituted the fruity, tropical Mole Manchamanteles for salsa. It's much more exciting!

In a small saucepan over low heat, gently warm the mole.

Add 1 teaspoon of the bacon grease to a cast-iron skillet over medium-low heat. Fry 1 tortilla on each side until warmed and softened. Transfer the tortilla to a plate. Repeat with the remaining grease and tortillas.

In the same skillet, fry the eggs, seasoning with salt and pepper.

In another skillet, heat the peas and ham.

On one serving plate, pour a dollop of the mole and top with a tortilla. Pour more mole over it, top with another tortilla, and pour more mole over that, spreading it over the surface of the tortilla.

Top each stack of tortillas with a fried egg. Garnish each with peas, ham, and cheese. If desired, serve alongside refried beans and plantains.

Chorizo and Mole Negro Breakfast Burritos

xxxxxx

Breakfast burritos, like regular burritos, are served two ways: wrapped in aluminum foil for on-the-go eating or on a plate to be conquered with a fork and knife. I think this recipe works best when served at the table, where the sauce can be appreciated by the eyes as well as the stomach.

Serves 4

¹/₂ pound chorizo (see Sources, page 86)

2 large potatoes, peeled and shredded

Salt and freshly ground black pepper

6 eggs

¹/₄ cup milk

1 ¹/₂ cups Mole Negro (see page 23)

4 large flour tortillas

1 cup grated asadero (see Sources, page 86) or Monterey Jack cheese

In a large, cast-iron skillet over medium heat, fry the chorizo until cooked through. Using a slotted spoon, transfer it to a paper-towel-lined plate to drain.

To the same skillet add the shredded potatoes; sprinkle with salt and pepper and cook, turning, until browned on both sides. Transfer the potatoes to a plate and cover loosely with foil to keep warm.

In a small bowl, beat the eggs with the milk. Cook the eggs in the skillet, using a heat-proof spatula to push the eggs around the bottom of the pan as they set. When they're cooked through but still soft, turn off the heat.

In a small saucepan over low heat, warm the mole.

Warm the tortillas, one by one, on a comal, or in a clean, dry skillet set over medium heat. Put ¼ of the sausage, potatoes, eggs, and cheese in a rectangular pile in the middle of a warmed tortilla. Fold the two short sides in towards the middle; fold the bottom up and over the filling, and roll towards the top. Repeat for the 3 remaining burritos. Pour ¼ of the warm mole over each burrito and serve.

Shredded Duck Quesadillas

xxxxxx

The prospect of leftover duck is a good enough reason to spend the effort making a dish like Orange-Honey Mole with Roast Duck (page 33). Although you will probably have devoured all of the breast and leg meat, there should still be enough meat on the carcass to make a few quesadillas. Save some of the Orange-Honey Mole for dipping sauce. Of course you can also use chicken with this, or another mole, for similar quesadillas.

Serves 4

5 teaspoons vegetable oil, divided

¹/₂ medium onion, thinly sliced

4 small flour tortillas

1 cup grated asadero cheese (see Sources, page 86)

1 large, ripe avocado, peeled, pitted, and sliced

1 cup cooked, shredded duck

¹/₄ cup chopped cilantro leaves

1 cup Orange-Honey Mole (see page 33)

In a cast-iron skillet, heat about 1 teaspoon of oil over medium heat and add the onion. Cook until it is softened and turns golden. Remove the onion from the skillet and set aside.

Add 1 teaspoon vegetable oil to the skillet, followed by 1 tortilla. Cook about 1 minute, until it turns light golden, then flip it.

Quickly sprinkle half of the tortilla with some of the onion, cheese, avocado slices, duck meat, and cilantro.

Fold the other half of the tortilla over the filling and gently press it down. Cook for about 2 minutes, until the cheese has partially melted. Turn and cook about 2 more minutes, until the cheese is fully melted.

Repeat with the remaining tortillas and serve immediately, with warmed Orange-Honey Mole as a dipping sauce.

Frito Pies

xxxxxx

Serves 4

1 pound ground beef

Salt and freshly ground black pepper

2 cups Mole Coloradito (see page 20) or Mole Rojo (see page 16)

10-ounce bag of Fritos

1/2 cup chopped white onion

1 cup shredded asadero cheese (see Sources, page 86) or Monterey Jack

The great Southwestern Frito Pie—found at fiestas, ball games, and diners—is traditionally made by splitting open a single-size bag of Fritos (no other corn chips will work), pouring in a ladleful of Texas chili, and adding a sprinkling of chopped onion and a handful of shredded Cheddar cheese. The weak link of the Frito Pie is often canned chili that is too salty, too fatty, and lacking any real flavor. This recipe replaces the chili with a beefy mole for a richer, hotter, and more complex pie.

Add the ground beef to a skillet over medium-high heat. Sprinkle with salt and pepper and cook through. Break up large chunks of meat, but don't stir too often or you'll prevent it from browning well.

Add the mole, reduce the heat, and simmer 20 minutes or until the mixture has thickened slightly.

Divide the Fritos evenly between four shallow bowls. Top with meat and mole mixture, onions, and cheese. Serve immediately.

Shrimp Flautas with Manchamanteles Dipping Sauce

xxxxxx

Makes 12

The chunkiness of Mole Manchamanteles is one of its most unique and attractive attributes, second only to its intoxicating tropical flavor. That flavor is a perfect match with these crispy rolled tacos filled with garlicky shrimp; the chunkiness, however, doesn't work. So for this recipe, the mole is pureed to make a smooth sauce that is a little bit less of a tablecloth-stainer.

To make the dipping sauce, puree the mole with the oregano. The easiest way to puree such a small amount is with a hand-held blender, but if you don't have one, use your regular blender. Season to taste with salt and pepper and set aside.

Into a large saucepan over medium-high heat, pour corn oil to a depth of 1½ inches. Bring the oil to 350 degrees F.

Meanwhile, melt the butter in a skillet. Add the shrimp and garlic and sauté until shrimp are just cooked through, about 3 minutes. Remove the skillet from the heat and allow the shrimp to cool slightly. Coarsely chop the shrimp and season to taste with salt and pepper.

Take one of the corn tortillas and dip it into the hot oil. Drain briefly on a paper towel. Spread a few teaspoons of the shrimp in a long, thin rectangle on the tortilla and roll it up like a cigarette. Secure the flap with a toothpick. Repeat with the remaining tortillas and shrimp filling.

Fry each flauta until golden, about 30 seconds. Drain on paper towels. Be sure to remove the toothpicks! Serve with warmed Manchamanteles Dipping Sauce.

1 cup Mole Manchamanteles (see page 26)

1 teaspoon dried Mexican oregano (see Sources, page 86)

Salt and freshly ground black pepper

Corn oil for frying

2 tablespoons butter

½ pound medium shrimp, shelled and deveined

1 teaspoon minced garlic

12 corn tortillas

Mashed Plantain Fritters
with Apple Butter Mole

xxxxxx

Makes 8–12

2 large, ripe plantains

Salt and freshly
ground black pepper

1/2 teaspoon baking powder

Peanut oil, lard,
or vegetable oil for frying

1 1/2 cups Apple Butter Mole
(see page 35)

These crispy fritters also pair well with Mole Manchamanteles or the Mild and Chunky Mole Amarillo.

Peel and slice the plantains lengthwise, into long planks. Put the plantain planks into a deep saucepan, and pour in enough water to cover. Bring to a boil, reduce heat, and simmer until tender, about 15 minutes.

Drain the plantains and transfer them to a large bowl. Mash until almost smooth. Season with salt and pepper, then sprinkle in the baking powder and mash again.

To form the fritters, take a heaping ¼ cup of batter and pat it into a little cake about ½ inch thick. Pour a thin layer of oil in a large skillet set over medium heat. Fry each patty, flipping once, until golden on both sides. Serve immediately.

Serve drizzled with warm mole or with the mole on the side, as a dipping sauce.

Squash Blossom Empanadas
xxxxxx

Empanadas filled with squash blossoms (flor de calabaza) *are a favorite street food in Oaxaca. But these are not the flaky pastry pockets you may be imagining; Oaxacan empanadas are more like quesadillas made by folding over a freshly made corn tortilla. You can double the recipe and serve them piled on a platter at a buffet, or make a small batch and serve them one to a plate, sitting in a puddle of mole amarillo and garnished with an extra blossom.*

In a large mixing bowl, work the butter into the masa harina and salt using a pastry blender or your hands. Add the vegetable stock or water and work into a firm dough. Divide the dough into 4 quarters. From each of the quarters roll 3 cherry-tomato-sized balls.

Flatten the balls into 6-inch discs using a tortilla press or a rolling pin (putting each ball between two pieces of waxed paper will help prevent sticking).

Cook the empanadas on a cast-iron skillet or comal over medium heat. First, place a tortilla on the comal and cook for 1 minute. Flip the tortilla and arrange on half of it 2 tablespoons shredded cheese, 2 squash blossoms, a few golden raisins, and a sprig of cilantro. Fold the other half over and use a fork to press the edges together, sealing it shut. Cook for about 3 minutes on each side, or until golden. Repeat with the remaining ingredients.

Serve empanadas drizzled with mole or sitting in a puddle of it.

Makes 12

2 tablespoons butter

2 cups masa harina
(see Sources, page 86)

1 teaspoon salt

1 cup vegetable stock
or water

1 1/2 cups shredded asadero
cheese (see Sources,
page 86)

24 squash blossoms

1/2 cup golden raisins

12 small sprigs cilantro

2 cups Saffron-Scented
Mole Amarillo, heated
(see page 29)

Wild Mushroom and Roasted Poblano Empanadas

xxxxxx

Makes 12

2 tablespoons butter

2 cups masa harina (see
Sources, page 86)

1 teaspoon salt

1 cup vegetable
stock or water

2 fresh poblano chiles

2 tablespoons lard
or vegetable oil

1/2 pound wild mushrooms,
brushed clean and chopped

1 teaspoon
minced garlic

Salt and freshly
ground pepper

1 1/2 cups crumbled cotija
cheese (see Sources,
page 86)

2 cups Mole Verde
(see page 19)

These, like the squash blossom empanadas, are like quesadillas made with small corn tortillas. Use whatever kind of wild mushrooms you can find in your market. I use a combination of chanterelles, oyster mushrooms, and morels. Don't be put off by the high price per pound of wild mushrooms. The last time I bought morels they were $59.99 per pound, but I got 6 or 7 of these big, lightweight mushrooms for just $6.

In a large mixing bowl, work the butter into the masa harina and salt using a pastry blender or your hands. Add the vegetable stock or water and work into a firm dough. Divide the dough into 4 quarters. From each of the quarters roll 3 cherry-tomato-sized balls.

Roast and peel the poblanos according to the directions on page 32 (Mild and Chunky Mole Amarillo recipe). Remove the stems and seeds, and finely chop the chiles.

In a cast-iron skillet over medium heat, melt the lard or oil and sauté the poblanos, mushrooms, and garlic together until the mushrooms release their juices. Remove from the heat and season to taste with salt and pepper.

Flatten the dough balls into 6-inch discs using a tortilla press or a rolling pin (putting each ball between two pieces of waxed paper will help prevent sticking).

Cook the empanadas on a cast-iron skillet or comal over medium heat. First, place a tortilla on the comal and cook for one minute. Flip the tortilla and arrange on half of it 2 tablespoons of the mushroom mixture and about 2 tablespoons cotija cheese. Fold the other half over and use a fork to press the edges together, sealing it shut. Fry for about 3 minutes on each side, or until golden. Repeat with the remaining ingredients.

Serve the empanadas drizzled with Mole Verde or sitting in a puddle of it.

Shredded Chicken Nachos

xxxxxx

When I get home from the grocery store with a hot rotisserie chicken, the first thing I do is rip off the salty, crispy skin in a single sheet. After that I usually go for the wings; they have a high skin-to-meat ratio. And after that, with most of the flavorful skin gone, I tend to lose interest in the bird. That is, until I get a hankering for something like chicken nachos. Denuded rotisserie chickens are the perfect source of ready-to-go chicken for a dish like this.

In a large, ovenproof serving dish, arrange half of the tortilla chips. Top with half of the chicken, beans, mole, and cheese. Repeat for the second layer, ending again with the cheese.

Broil for 3–5 minutes, until the cheese is melted.

Top with salsa and serve.

Serves 4–6

14-ounce bag of tortilla chips

1 1/2 cups shredded chicken

1 1/2 cups refried black beans, heated through

1 cup Mole Poblano, heated (see page 24)

2 cups shredded asadero cheese (see Sources, page 86)

1 cup fresh salsa

Chicken Wings in Mole

xxxxxx

Serves 8

4 pounds chicken wings

**Salt and freshly
ground pepper**

4 cups mole

**¹/₄ cup toasted
sesame seeds**

These wings are perfect party food. They're easy to make ahead of time, and people love them. Orange-Honey Mole (see page 33), Mole Coloradito (page 20), Mole Rojo made with dried cranberries (page 16), and Mole Poblano (page 24) all work well for this recipe.

Arrange the chicken wings in 2 shallow baking pans. Sprinkle liberally with salt and pepper. Broil for 10–15 minutes, turning once, until the wings are golden and crispy.

Transfer the wings to a large, deep saucepan or Dutch oven and pour the mole over them. Add water as necessary to thin the mole enough to cover the wings. Bring to a boil, reduce heat, and simmer 30 minutes. Sprinkle with toasted sesame seeds and serve.

Sesame-Crusted Red Snapper Soft Tacos with Mild and Chunky Mole Amarillo

xxxxxx

If you're making this dish the same day you're making the mole, feel free to leave the sesame seeds out of the mole recipe, as they're used here as a coating for the fish. If you're using leftover mole, then don't worry about it. There's no such thing as too many toasted sesame seeds!

Cut the snapper fillets into pieces about 1 x 4 inches each.

Heat the vegetable oil in a skillet over medium heat.

Sprinkle the fish on both sides with salt and pepper. Pour the sesame seeds onto a plate and press the top and bottom of each piece of snapper into the seeds. In the heated skillet, fry the fish about 3 minutes on each side or until cooked through. Drain the fish on paper towels.

In a clean skillet or on a comal, warm the tortillas, two or three at a time. Fill each warmed tortilla with 1 or 2 pieces of fish, top with the mole and cilantro, and serve immediately.

Serves 4

1 $1/2$ pounds red snapper

2 tablespoons vegetable oil

Salt and freshly ground pepper

$1/3$ cup white and/or black sesame seeds

12 corn tortillas

2 cups Mild and Chunky Mole Amarillo, cold or room-temperature (see page 32)

12 sprigs fresh cilantro

Pork Flatbread Sandwiches with Mole Verde

xxxxxx

Serves 4

1 1/2 pounds pork, cut into 1-inch cubes

1 tablespoon Mexican oregano (see Sources, page 86)

1 teaspoon ground cumin

1 tablespoon red pepper flakes

1/2 teaspoon salt

Freshly ground black pepper

2 tablespoons olive oil

1 red onion, cut into 1-inch squares

4 large pieces flatbread

1 1/2 cups Mole Verde (see page 19), cold or at room temperature

2 medium tomatoes, cut into thin wedges

Shredded lettuce

This is the same concept as the Greek souvlaki, in which seasoned cubes of grilled pork and vegetables are drizzled with a thick sauce and served tucked in a piece of fluffy flatbread. In this case, the thick sauce is a spicy mole verde. The best flatbreads to use for this sandwich are freshly baked pita bread, Afghan bread, or Indian naan. You can ask for an extra order or two of such bread to go next time you visit your favorite restaurant, or look for them in the frozen section of your international foods store. Thick, homemade flour tortillas also work well.

In a large bowl, toss the pork with the oregano, cumin, red pepper flakes, salt, pepper, and olive oil. Cover with plastic wrap and refrigerate overnight.

When you're ready to cook the meat, preheat your gas or charcoal grill to medium-high.

Meanwhile, thread alternating chunks of pork and onion onto 4 metal skewers. (I find that even if you soak bamboo skewers in water, they always seem to burn.)

Grill the kebabs for about 10 minutes, turning them at least twice. You can move the skewers to a cooler part of the grill if they start to burn. Remove them from the grill when the cubes of pork are firm, but the meat is still slightly rosy inside.

Heat the flatbreads briefly on the grill. Pull the meat and onions from each skewer onto a flatbread, top with mole, tomatoes, and shredded lettuce, and serve.

Golden Tamales with Saffron-Scented Mole Amarillo

xxxxxx

Tamales, like mole, are very labor-intensive. Do yourself a favor and don't plan to make mole and tamales all in one day— unless you have a house full of willing helpers. This recipe makes about 12 tamales, enough to serve a minimum of 6 hungry people as a main course or 12 people as part of a larger meal. Do not immediately reject the idea of using lard for these tamales; it really does produce the lightest, fluffiest dough.

Put the dried corn husks in a tall pitcher or vase and pour hot water over them so they'll soften while you make the dough.

In a small saucepan, bring the water or chicken stock to a boil, then remove it from the heat and add azafrán.

In the workbowl of your standing electric mixer, beat the lard or butter with the paddle attachment until light and fluffy. Continue beating on low while you slowly add the masa harina and salt. Pour in enough chicken stock to make the dough moist but not wet. It should pull away from the walls of the workbowl but not stick to the paddle in one big clump. Let the dough rest for 30 minutes.

Serves at least 6

24 dried corn husks (see Sources, page 86)

2 cups water or chicken stock

1/2 teaspoon Mexican azafrán (see Sources, page 86)

1 cup lard or unsalted butter

3 cups masa harina (see Sources, page 86)

1 teaspoon salt

1 cup cooked, shredded chicken, duck, or pork

1/4 cup golden raisins

4 cups Saffron-Scented Mole Amarillo, warmed (see page 29)

Salt and pepper

(If you don't have a standing mixer, you can beat the lard with a handheld mixer; do the rest of the mixing by hand. If you don't have a mixer, you can simply use softened lard and work it in by hand. The results will just be more dense.)

To make the filling: In a small bowl, combine the shredded meat and raisins. Add just enough mole to moisten the mixture. It shouldn't be soupy. Season to taste with salt and pepper.

Remove 1 husk from the soaking water and shake off any excess water. Lay the husk flat on a work surface. Scoop about ¼ cup of the masa from the bowl and spread it out on the middle of the husk in roughly the shape of a rectangle. Put about 1 tablespoon of the shredded meat filling in a narrower rectangle in the middle of the masa. Lift the sides of the husk together towards the middle, enclosing the filling with masa. Drop the sides. Fold the bottom of the husk up over the filling and the top of the husk down. Rotate the tamal and fold the sides in over the center. Now tear a long strip from one of the softened husks and use it to tie a "belt" around the middle of the folded tamal. Repeat until all of the masa is used.

Fill the bottom of your steamer with water and bring to a boil. Put the tamales on the rack of the steamer and cook 1 hour, or until they are puffed and firm. (If you don't have a steamer, simply wad up 6 or so balls of tin foil and put them in the bottom of a large stockpot and use it as a rack.)

Serve the tamales hot and still wrapped, with the rest of the mole on the side.

Iliana de la Vega's Mole Coloradito

xxxxxx

Chef Iliana de la Vega offers cooking classes at her attractive Restaurante El Naranjo in Oaxaca City, Mexico. She has been featured in the New York Times *and* Bon Appétit. *If you can't find Oaxacan oregano* (Lippia berliandieri) *you can substitute Mexican oregano, or Greek oregano and a pinch of marjoram.*

Bring to a boil 2 quarts of water, then add the onion, 3 cloves of garlic, and salt to taste. Next, add the chicken or other meat pieces, reduce the heat, and simmer until the meat is done. Remove the meat pieces, strain the broth, and reserve.

To make the mole: In a medium cast-iron skillet over high heat, dry-roast the tomatoes and the unpeeled garlic cloves until black spots just begin to show. Remove the garlic and continue to roast the tomatoes until they are soft and blistered. Peel the garlic cloves and reserve both the tomatoes and the garlic.

Discard the seeds and stems from the chiles. In a separate skillet, roast them slightly until black spots begin to show, or until they soften—not too long, just a few seconds on each side. Then transfer them to a pot containing hot water to cover and let them soak for no more than 20 minutes.

Add 1½ tablespoons of oil to a skillet and fry the bread until pale gold. Add the blanched almonds, sesame seeds, oregano, peppercorns, and cloves, and fry over high heat just until they are pale gold and aromatic; reserve. Dry-roast the canela separately and reserve.

Serves 8

½ medium white onion

3 cloves garlic

Salt

8 pieces chicken (or servings of beef, venison, pork, or turkey)

4 large Roma tomatoes

4 medium cloves garlic, unpeeled

10 dry ancho chiles

1 dry pasilla chile

3 tablespoons vegetable oil, divided

2 slices day-old bread (not flavored or sweet)

15 blanched almonds

½ cup sesame seeds

1 tablespoon dry Oaxacan oregano

10 black peppercorns

3 whole cloves

1-inch piece of canela (see Sources, page 86)

1 cup chicken or vegetable broth

3 tablespoons sugar (or to taste)

Meanwhile, heat the rest of the oil in a big pot over medium-low heat. Drain the chiles by scooping them up carefully, and discard the water, which may contain dust and pesticides. Blend the chiles with enough fresh water to make a smooth puree, add the puree to the pot, and let it fry for about 8–10 minutes.

Then blend the reserved nuts and spices, the tomatoes, and the garlic with enough water to make a puree, and add to the cooking pot. Separately, blend the canela with a little water and pass this mixture through a sieve over the mole.

Let the mole simmer for approximately 20 minutes, or until it is thickened. Then add the chicken or vegetable broth and bring to a boil. Let it cook for another 15 minutes and season to taste with salt and sugar. The mole should be thick enough to coat the back of a spoon, and it should not be overly sweet. Now add the chicken or other meat, let it simmer for 10 minutes, and serve with rice and warm corn tortillas.

Turkey Mole Burgers

xxxxx

Serves 4

3 tablespoons
store-bought mole paste
$1/3$ cup warm water
$1 1/2$ pounds ground turkey
Red chile powder (optional)
4 flour tortillas or rolls
$1/4$ cup mayonnaise
Iceberg lettuce leaves
Tomato slices

Store-bought mole delivers a quick dose of flavor to turkey, which can be dry and bland. Look for jars of mole in the Mexican foods section of your supermarket. Popular brands include Doña Maria, Rogelio Bueno, and El Mexicano. I like to wrap these burgers up in warm, fluffy, freshly made flour tortillas, but you also can use Mexican bolillos or other buns.

Preheat a charcoal or gas grill to high heat.

In a small bowl, whisk together the mole paste and warm water until it is the consistency of a thick sauce.

In a large bowl, combine the turkey and mole sauce. If you like your mole hot, add some of your favorite kind of red chile powder. Gently form into 4 patties.

Grill the burgers over high heat until they reach your desired level of doneness. Remove the burgers and warm the tortillas or rolls briefly on the grill.

Spread about 1 tablespoon of mayonnaise on the center of each tortilla or bun. Top with iceberg lettuce, tomato slices, and a hot burger. If you are using tortillas, fold the tortilla up around the burger. Serve immediately.

Calabacitas Burritos

XXXXXX

Calabacitas is a dish of summer squash fried with corn and chiles. Mexican summer squash is a mottled green and milder and sweeter than zucchini or yellow squash, although you can use any kind of summer squash for this recipe. If you're not a vegetarian, try making this dish with bacon grease instead of butter. It's spectacular!

In a large skillet over medium heat, melt the butter or bacon grease. Add the onion and cook until softened. Add the squash and garlic, and stir to combine. Cook, covered, about 10 minutes. Add corn and poblano chiles and continue cooking, uncovered, until the squash is tender. Season to taste with salt and pepper. Set aside.

Warm the tortillas, one by one, on a comal, or in a clean, dry skillet set over medium heat. Put ¼ of the vegetable mixture, cheese, cilantro, and mole in a rectangular pile in the middle of a warmed tortilla. Fold the two short sides in towards the middle; fold the bottom up and over the filling, and roll towards the top. Repeat for the remaining burritos.

Serves 4–6

2 tablespoons butter

1 small white onion, peeled and diced

2 Mexican summer squash (about $1/2$ pound each), diced

2 cloves garlic, minced

2 large ears fresh corn (about $1 1/2$ cups kernels)

2 roasted and peeled poblano chiles, chopped

Salt and pepper

4 flour tortillas (12-inch size)

1 cup shredded asadero cheese (see Sources, page 86) or Monterey Jack

$1/2$ cup chopped cilantro leaves

1 cup Mole Verde, cold or room-temperature (see page 19)

Mole Poblano Enchilada Casserole

xxxxxx

Serves 4

Vegetable oil for frying

12 corn tortillas

$1/2$ cup finely chopped onion

2 cups shredded turkey

$1 1/2$ cups shredded asadero cheese (see Sources, page 86) or Monterey Jack

2 cups Nancy's Mole Poblano (see page 24)

$1-1 1/2$ cups Mexican crema or thin sour cream

Chopped fresh cilantro, chopped onions, sliced radishes, sliced avocados, grated cotija cheese (or more of the above cheeses), for garnish

This is one of the ways that Nancy Gerlach dresses up leftover Thanksgiving turkey. It is adapted from the version that appears in The Spicy Food Lover's Bible. *You can also substitute shredded chicken, whether from leftover grilled chicken breasts or a store-bought rotisserie chicken.*

Preheat oven to 350 degrees F and oil an 8 x 8-inch baking dish.

Add oil to a depth of ½ inch in a small, heavy skillet set over medium heat. When hot, quickly fry each tortilla, one at a time, to soften, about 5 or 10 seconds on each side. Do not fry until crisp! Drain on paper towels and drain off all but a teaspoon of oil.

To the same skillet, add the onions and sauté until soft. Combine the onion, turkey, and shredded cheese in a bowl and toss.

To assemble the casserole, spoon a couple of tablespoons of mole in the bottom of the casserole and top with 4 of the tortillas. Spread some of the turkey mixture on the tortillas and top with a layer of crema, add another layer of tortillas, then turkey and crema, and end with a layer of tortillas.

Pour the remaining mole over the casserole and bake, uncovered, for 20 minutes.

Remove from the oven and let stand 10 minutes to set. Serve garnished with cilantro, onions, radishes, avocados, and a sprinkle of grated cheese.

Bride's Mole Pasta

xxxxxx

This recipe came about on a late night when I was too hungry to think straight. There was very little food in the house and, well, you know how that goes. Hunger acquaints a pan with strange bedfellows. Bride's Mole is something for which I've never seen a recipe, but I found a bottle of it in a Hispanic food shop in Santa Fe. The maker is Cocina Mestiza, and their bottled mole pastes are the best I've tasted in the U.S. As this recipe proves, they're quite versatile.

Cook the noodles according to the package instructions and drain.

Meanwhile, in a small saucepan over medium-low heat, combine Bride's Mole with chicken stock and cook, whisking, until the sauce thickens, about 5 minutes.

In a skillet over medium-high heat, fry the meat until browned and cooked through. Using a slotted spoon, remove the meat to a bowl and cover to keep warm.

Reduce heat to medium, add the onions and mushrooms to the meat drippings, and cook until the onions soften and mushrooms release their juices. Add the reserved meat and mole sauce to the onions and mushrooms, stirring to combine. Reduce heat to low and cook gently for 5 minutes. Season to taste with salt and pepper.

Pour sauce over pasta and serve.

Serves 4–6

1 pound rigatoni or egg noodles

$1/4$ jar Bride's Mole (see Sources, page 86)

$1 1/2$ cups chicken stock

1 pound ground beef, veal, or pork

$1/2$ medium onion, halved and sliced into $1/4$-inch ribs

$1/2$ pound mushrooms, brushed clean and sliced

Salt and freshly ground pepper

Monkfish Braised in Saffron-Scented Mole Amarillo

xxxxxx

What is monkfish? It is the ugliest fish you've never seen. If you came across one on a mucky seafloor, it would surely ruin your appetite. And yet the flavor of this hideous beast is simply beautiful—sweet and rich, with a dense, meaty texture. It is often compared to lobster and it's no wonder why the flavors are similar: monkfish literally eat lobster for breakfast.

In a large, heavy-bottomed saucepan or Dutch oven over medium-high heat, melt the lard or heat the vegetable oil.

Sprinkle the fish on both sides with salt and pepper and brown the fillets (about 2 minutes on each side). Add the mole and bring to a boil. Reduce heat and gently simmer until the fish is cooked through, 10–15 minutes. Serve the fish on a bed of rice or sautéed vegetables, with extra mole ladled over the top.

Serves 4–6

2 tablespoons lard or vegetable oil

1 1/2–2 pounds monkfish, cut into 4–6 fillets

Salt and freshly ground black pepper

4 cups thin Saffron-Scented Mole Amarillo (see page 29)

Rabbit in Mole Negro

xxxxxx

Serves 2–4

2 tablespoons lard
or vegetable oil

1 rabbit (about 3 pounds),
cut into 6–8 pieces

Salt and freshly
ground pepper

4 cups Mole Negro, plus
water to thin (see page 23)

My mother is a big fan of rabbit meat, and she encouraged me to use it instead of chicken for this recipe (although chicken works just fine). If you live in the city, look for rabbit meat at specialty butchers, European markets, and natural foods stores such as Whole Foods. If you live in the country, inquire among your neighbors; rabbits (like fast-growing zucchini) are often given gladly by those who raise them.

In a large Dutch oven over medium-high heat, melt the lard or heat the vegetable oil. Sprinkle the meat liberally with salt and pepper, and brown the rabbit pieces on all sides, working in batches if necessary.

Pour the mole over the meat, reduce heat, and simmer until the meat is cooked through, about 30 minutes.

I like to serve this with white rice, refried beans, and fresh peas.

Last-Minute Barbecue Sauce

XXXXXX

If you happen to reach into the refrigerator for barbecue sauce only to find none, don't fret. Assuming your fridge is otherwise well stocked with condiments, you can whip up this sauce in about 5 minutes. Slather it on any grilled or smoked meats about 5 minutes before they're done cooking and serve more of it on the side.

In a saucepan, combine the mole paste, marmalade, ketchup, cider vinegar, and chile. Whisk in the water. Bring to a boil over medium heat, reduce heat to low, and simmer 5 minutes, whisking often, until it thickens.

Makes about 2 cups

$1/3$ cup Rogelio Bueno or other store-bought mole paste

$1/3$ cup orange marmalade

$2/3$ cup ketchup

1 tablespoon cider vinegar

1 chipotle in adobo, finely chopped

2 cups water

South-of-the-Border Sloppy Joes

XXXXXX

After you've tried these "Mole Joes," you'll wonder why any-one bothers to make regular old Sloppy Joes.

Add the ground beef to a skillet set over medium-high heat. Sprinkle with salt and pepper and cook through. Break up large chunks of meat, but don't stir too often or it won't brown well.

Add the mole, reduce the heat, and simmer 20 minutes or until the mixture has thickened.

Put one bottom half of a roll on each plate and top with a mound of the Mole Joe mixture. Top with lettuce, tomatoes, and onions, and serve.

Serves 4

$1 1/2$ pounds ground beef

Salt and freshly ground black pepper

$1 1/2$–2 cups Mole Rojo (see page 16) or Mole Coloradito (see page 20)

4 Mexican bolillos or other substantial rolls, split and toasted

Bibb lettuce

Sliced tomatoes

Thinly sliced onions

Chicken Mole Soup with Masa Dumplings

xxxxxx

Serves 4–6

½ cup masa harina (see Sources, page 86)

½ teaspoon salt, plus more for the soup

¼ cup warm water

½ tablespoon lard

4 cups Saffron-Scented Mole Amarillo (see page 29)

3 cups chicken stock

2 ears fresh corn, shucked and sliced into ½-inch rounds

¼ pound green beans, trimmed and cut into 2-inch lengths

2 cups cooked, shredded chicken

½ cup chopped cilantro leaves

I wish I had known enough to ask for a stew like this when I was sick as a kid. It beats the pants off chicken noodle soup. The base of this soup is the thick, intensely flavored Saffron-Scented Mole Amarillo. Used in this way, it becomes much more subtle in combination with the other ingredients.

To make the dumplings: In a large bowl, mix together the masa harina and salt. Add the warm water and stir until combined. Mix in the lard.

To form the dumplings, take a small lump of dough and roll it into a ball about 1 inch in diameter. Holding the ball in the palm of one hand, use the thumb of your other hand to make a deep dimple in the ball. Repeat for the remaining dumplings. Let them rest 1 hour, covered with a damp dish towel.

While the dumplings are resting, combine the mole and stock in a large stockpot. Bring the mixture to a boil, add corn, green beans, and dumplings, and gently simmer for 15 minutes, until dumplings are cooked through. Add the chicken and simmer 5 more minutes.

Season to taste with salt, garnish with cilantro, and serve.

Grilled Flank Steak with Mole Verde

xxxxxx

I love the flavor of flank steak, a rather tough cut that comes, literally, from the belly of the beast. If you have leftover slices of steak, reheat them in a pan, toss with any mole, and tuck into a toasted bun for a quick and tasty sandwich.

Using a mortar and pestle, crush the garlic and salt into a paste. In a small bowl, combine the garlic paste, cumin, oregano, black pepper, and olive oil.

Lay the flank steak on a cutting board and make a series of shallow, crisscrossed cuts on the surface of the meat; flip and repeat on the other side. This will help the marinade penetrate and keep the meat from curling on the grill.

Rub the meat all over with the garlic and herb mixture and put it in a resealable plastic container or large zippered storage bag. Allow the meat to rest in the refrigerator 2 hours or overnight.

Preheat your grill to high heat. Leave the meat in the refrigerator until just before you put it on the grill. Grill to medium rare, about 4–5 minutes on each side. Transfer the steak to a platter, cover with foil, and allow it to rest 10 minutes.

Meanwhile, in a small saucepan, reheat the Mole Verde.

Slice the flank steak against the grain, into thin strips. Serve drizzled with mole.

Serves 4

6 cloves garlic, minced

1 teaspoon salt

2 tablespoons ground cumin

1 tablespoon dried Mexican oregano (see Sources, page 86)

1 teaspoon freshly ground black pepper

1 tablespoon olive oil

1 1/2 pounds flank steak

2 cups Mole Verde (see page 19)

Turkey Cutlets with Cranberry Mandarin Mole Sauce

xxxxxx

This recipe makes good use of a small amount of leftover mole. With the addition of orange juice and segments, it becomes a little lighter and a little sweeter, but still spicy and complex. Serve this with wild rice pilaf, fresh corn tamales, or herbed polenta.

In a small saucepan, combine the mole and mandarin orange segments, along with their juice. Bring the mixture to a boil, reduce heat, and simmer until thickened. Season to taste with salt.

Put each turkey breast between two pieces of heavy-duty plastic wrap and, using a kitchen mallet or similar blunt object, pound to a thickness of ½ inch.

Combine the coriander, cumin, salt, and pepper in a small bowl. Dust each piece of turkey on both sides with the spice mixture.

Add the vegetable oil to a cast-iron skillet over medium-high heat. Fry the cutlets until golden brown and crispy on both sides, 3–4 minutes total.

Serve topped with sauce.

Serves 4

$1/2$ cup Mole Rojo made with cranberries (see page 16)

1 small can mandarin orange segments

Salt

4 turkey breasts

1 teaspoon ground coriander

1 teaspoon ground cumin

1 teaspoon salt

1 teaspoon freshly ground pepper

1 tablespoon vegetable oil

Pozole with Mole Coloradito

xxxxxx

Serves 4

1 tablespoon lard or
vegetable oil

1 pound pork butt,
cut into 1 1/2-inch cubes

1 teaspoon minced garlic

1 white onion, peeled
and diced

1 tablespoon Mexican
oregano (see Sources,
page 86)

2 cans hominy
(15 ounces each)

6 cups chicken
stock

Salt

1–2 cups Mole Rojo
(see page 16) or Mole
Coloradito (see page 20),
heated

Pozole, a stew made with hominy, can be made with red or green chiles. Instead of cooking dried chiles with the hominy, this recipe uses mole for a quick but deeply flavored version of the stew.

Melt the lard or heat the vegetable oil in a large stockpot over medium-high heat. Add the pork and brown the cubes on all sides. Add garlic and onion, and cook about 2 minutes. Add the oregano, hominy, and stock and bring to a boil. Reduce heat and simmer about 20 minutes or until pork is cooked through. Season to taste with salt.

Serve with Mole Rojo or Mole Coloradito on the side, allowing guests to add as much as they like to the stew.

Steak and Cactus Burritos

xxxxxx

Men love these burritos. There's something about the combination of grilled beef and crunchy cactus strips (called nopalitos) that makes city slickers want to wear cowboy boots, grow beards, and rustle cattle. If you've got some vegetarian cowboys in your party, you can substitute grilled portobello mushrooms for steak.

Serves 4

1 large cactus paddle (prickly pear pad)

1 1/2 pounds bottom round steak

Salt and freshly ground pepper

1 cup Mole Verde (see page 19)

4 large flour tortillas

2 cups cooked black beans

1 cup crumbled cotija cheese

Preheat your grill to medium-high heat. Carefully remove all of the spines from the cactus paddle by holding the paddle firmly with tongs while cutting off the spines with a vegetable peeler. Put the paddle on the grill.

Sprinkle the steak all over with salt and pepper, and put it on the grill. Cook the steak and cactus paddle side-by-side, turning frequently, until the meat is cooked to medium rare and the cactus paddle is tender.

Transfer the steak and the cactus paddle to a cutting board. Let the steak rest, covered with aluminum foil, while you cut the cactus into nopalitos: strips about the size and shape of a green bean.

In a small saucepan, heat the Mole Verde.

Slice the beef as thin as you can with the sharpest knife you've got.

In a cast-iron skillet or comal over medium heat, warm the flour tortillas, flipping frequently, until they puff slightly. Take

1 warmed tortilla and arrange about ½ cup black beans in a rectangular pile in the middle of it. Top with ¼ of the grilled steak, ¼ of the nopalitos, and ¼ cup of the Mole Verde. Sprinkle with cheese. Fold the two short sides in towards the middle; fold the bottom up and over the filling, and roll towards the top. Repeat for the 3 remaining burritos.

Tropical Shrimp Burritos

xxxxxx

Serves 4

1 pound medium shrimp with shells on

1 tablespoon lime juice

1 tablespoon vegetable oil

Salt and freshly ground pepper

1 cup Mole Manchamanteles (see page 26)

4 large flour tortillas

1½ cups cooked black beans

1½ cups cooked rice

I love the flavor of shrimp and pineapple together. In this burrito, grilled shrimp get a kick from fruity, chunky Mole Manchamanteles. Grilling shrimp with their shells on adds flavor and prevents them from sticking.

In a large bowl, toss the shrimp with lime juice, vegetable oil, salt, and pepper. Allow to marinate while the grill heats up.

Heat your grill to medium-high heat.

Put the shrimp on skewers and grill until just cooked, about 2 minutes on each side. Remove from the heat.

In a small saucepan, heat the Mole Manchamanteles.

In a cast-iron skillet or comal over medium heat, warm the flour tortillas, flipping frequently, until they puff slightly. Take 1 warmed tortilla and arrange about ½ cup black beans in a rectangular pile in the middle of it. Top with ¼ of the cooked rice, ¼ of the shrimp, and ¼ cup of the Mole Manchamanteles. Fold the two short sides in towards the middle; fold the bottom up and over the filling, and roll towards the top. Repeat for the 3 remaining burritos.

Salmon in Banana Leaves

xxxxxx

Banana leaves are often used to wrap tamales in Mexico, and in Thailand they are most often used to wrap fish. I like to use Mole Manchamanteles for this recipe, but salmon also pairs well with Mole Verde and Orange-Honey Mole.

Preheat your grill to medium-high heat.

Wash and pat dry 1 large banana leaf. If necessary, trim it to approximately 1 foot by 2 feet. While you're at it, cut off one long, skinny piece to use for tying up the package.

Put the salmon, skin-side down, in the middle of the banana leaf. Sprinkle liberally with salt, pepper, and lime zest and juice.

Wrap the salmon as if the banana leaf were aluminum foil and you were preparing it for the freezer. (Try to remember which side is up so that you can present the salmon at the table with the skin side down.) Tie the packet securely with the long strip of banana leaf.

Put the packet, skin-side down, on the grill and cook 10–12 minutes, or until your desired level of doneness. Transfer the packet to a serving platter. Using a sharp knife, cut through the banana leaf to expose the fish. Present it this way at the table, alongside a bowl of warmed Mole Manchamanteles.

Serves 4–6

1 package frozen banana leaves (see Sources, page 86)

$1 1/2$ pounds salmon, skin on if possible

Salt and freshly ground pepper

Zest and juice of 1 lime

$2 1/2$ cups Mole Manchamanteles, heated (see page 26)

Pan-Seared Scallops with White Chocolate Mole

xxxxxx

Serves 4–6

4 tablespoons unsalted butter, divided

$1/2$ small white onion, halved and thinly sliced

1 large carrot, cut into matchstick-size strips

1 zucchini, cut into matchstick-size strips

Salt and freshly ground pepper

1–1$1/2$ pounds sea scallops

1 teaspoon or more ground coriander

3 cups White Chocolate Mole (see page 36)

4–6 cups cooked white rice

It is hard to imagine scallops tasting better than they do simply slathered with garlic butter, but they are outrageously good with decadent White Chocolate Mole.

Melt 2 tablespoons of the butter in a large skillet over medium heat. Add the onion and sauté until softened. Add the carrot and stir to combine. Cover and cook about 3 minutes. Add the zucchini and sauté, uncovered, until all the vegetables are tender, about 3 minutes. Transfer the vegetables to a bowl, season to taste with salt and pepper, and cover loosely with plastic wrap.

Return the skillet to the heat and add the remaining 2 tablespoons butter. Increase the heat to medium-high and sauté the scallops, turning once, until cooked through, about 5 minutes. Unless you have a very large skillet, you'll have to do this in batches. Transfer the cooked scallops to a bowl and toss with salt, pepper, and ground coriander, to taste.

In a saucepan over low heat, gently warm the White Chocolate Mole.

Put equal portions of white rice on plates. Top with scallops, vegetables, and White Chocolate Mole. Serve immediately.

Fruit ices offer a light, tart finish to a meal enriched by mole.
Zapote, a plumlike tropical fruit (above), is a special favorite in
Mexico, but pineapple, mango, lime, lemon, peach, and berry
sorbets are also deliciously refreshing.

Grilled Banana Splits with Fiery Chocolate Sauce

xxxxxx

I toyed with the idea of using real mole for this dish and quickly thought better of it. Banana splits require a sauce made mostly of chocolate, with perhaps a dash of chile, whereas mole is mostly chile with perhaps a dash of chocolate. But the combination of toasted nuts, smoky chile, and creamy chocolate is still here, and it is delicious over sweet grilled bananas. If you can find baby bananas in the market, try using them to make small, individual splits.

Preheat your grill to medium-high heat.

To make the sauce: Use a double boiler if you have one. If not, pour water to a depth of 3 inches in a saucepan and bring it to a simmer. Set over the saucepan a stainless steel bowl, making sure the bottom of the bowl does not touch the water below. (If it does, pour out some of the water.)

Add both kinds of chocolate to the bowl and stir as it melts. The chocolate chips will melt smoothly, but the grainy Mexican chocolate will just become soft. When all the chocolate is soft, add the cream in a slow, steady stream, whisking constantly. Add the chile powder and continue whisking until all of the chocolate is dissolved and the sauce has thickened. Remove from the heat.

Slice the unpeeled bananas in half lengthwise and brush the cut sides lightly with oil. Make sure your grill grate is clean, and brush it with oil. Put the bananas, cut sides down, on the grate

Serves 4

3-ounce tablet of Mexican drinking chocolate, broken up

$1/2$ cup dark or semisweet chocolate chips

$1/2$ cup heavy cream

$1/4$–$1/2$ teaspoon chipotle powder or cayenne

4 small, ripe bananas (peels on)

Canola oil, for grilling

1 pint vanilla or coconut ice cream

1 cup crushed roasted peanuts, almonds, and/or pecans

Whipped cream

and cook until browned, about 2 minutes. Flip the bananas and cook 2 minutes more. Remove from the grill and peel as soon as they're cool enough to touch.

In a small bowl, arrange two banana halves. Top with scoops of ice cream, Fiery Chocolate Sauce, crushed nuts, and whipped cream.

Ray's White Mole Ice Cream

xxxxxx

Makes 1 quart

1 cup water

3 dried ancho chiles, stemmed and seeded

6 ounces high-quality white chocolate, broken into small pieces

2 cups milk

2 cups heavy cream

$3/4$ cup sugar

1 vanilla bean

$1/2$ teaspoon freshly ground cinnamon

$1/4$ teaspoon freshly ground cloves

$1/4$ teaspoon freshly ground pepper

6 egg yolks

Is this mole? Not really, but it incorporates many of the same flavors. This is my adaptation of a recipe invented by my buddy Ray Lampe, aka Dr. BBQ. The original version appears in his book Dr. BBQ's Barbecue All Year Long Cookbook.

In a saucepan over high heat, bring the water to a boil.

In a cast-iron skillet over medium heat, toast the chiles on both sides until they soften slightly and become aromatic. Transfer the chiles to a medium-sized, heat-safe bowl and pour in enough hot water to cover. Keep the chiles submerged with a small plate or saucer. Allow to soak for about 15 minutes, then puree completely in a blender.

Use a double boiler or pour water to a depth of 3 inches in a saucepan and bring it to a simmer. Set over the saucepan a stainless steel bowl, making sure the bottom of the bowl does not touch the water below. (If it does, pour out some of the water.) In the bowl, melt the chocolate, stirring constantly. The bottom of the bowl should be about 2 inches above the surface of the water.

In a medium saucepan over medium heat, combine the milk, cream, and sugar. Bring it to a boil, then turn off the heat. Split the vanilla bean and scrape all of the seeds into the pan. Add the cinnamon, cloves, and pepper.

Add the egg yolks to a mixing bowl and pour in about ⅓ of the hot milk mixture while whisking constantly. Return the milk and cream mixture to the heat and whisk in the egg yolk mixture. Cook 1 minute, whisking constantly.

Pour the mixture through a fine sieve into a large bowl. Stir in the chiles and melted chocolate and chill completely, or freeze in an ice-cream maker according to the manufacturer's instructions.

Chocolate Chile Pepita Cookies

xxxxxx

Makes 1½–2 dozen

1 ½ cups shelled pepitas

1 cup all-purpose flour

½ teaspoon ground cinnamon

1 pinch ground cloves

1 teaspoon cayenne pepper

½ teaspoon baking soda

¼ teaspoon salt

½ cup butter, room temperature

¾ cup golden-brown sugar

1 ½ teaspoons vanilla extract

¼ teaspoon almond extract

1 large egg

6 ounces semisweet chocolate, roughly chopped

These crunchy cookies will make regular chocolate chip cookies seem boring by comparison. They make fantastic ice cream sandwiches when filled with a scoop of Häagen-Dazs dulce de leche ice cream.

Preheat oven to 350 degrees F.

In a blender or food processor, process the pepitas until coarse. Transfer to a large mixing bowl. Add the flour, cinnamon, cloves, cayenne, baking soda, and salt, and stir to combine.

In the workbowl of your standing mixer, or using a handheld electric mixer and a large bowl, beat together the butter, brown sugar, vanilla, and almond extract. Add the egg and beat until fluffy. Add the flour mixture a little at a time and beat until combined. Using a sturdy spoon, mix in the chocolate chunks.

Drop dough by the heaping tablespoon onto a baking sheet, spacing cookies about 2 inches apart.

Bake until golden, about 10–12 minutes. Remove from oven and let rest until cookies are set, then transfer cookies from the baking sheet to a rack and allow to cool completely.

Individual Chocolate Mole Cakes

xxxxxx

Makes 8 cakes

11 ounces bittersweet chocolate, roughly chopped

10 tablespoons (1 1/4 sticks) unsalted butter

1/2 dried pasilla chile, stemmed and seeded (see Sources, page 86)

1/2 dried ancho chile, stemmed and seeded (see Sources, page 86)

10 tablespoons sugar

2-inch piece of canela (see Sources, page 86)

1/4 teaspoon ground cloves

2 tablespoons hulled pumpkin seeds

9 large eggs

1/2 tablespoon pure vanilla extract

Southwestern chef Stephan Pyles created this recipe, which appears in his book Southwestern Vegetarian. *He serves the cakes with cherry-almond ice cream, tamarind anglaise, and orange caramel sauce, and no doubt it is delicious that way, but I've never had the patience to make all that stuff in one day. I think the little cakes are delicious simply served warm and topped with a scoop of ice cream.*

Preheat the oven to 300 degrees F.

Use a double boiler or pour water to a depth of 3 inches in a saucepan and bring it to a simmer. Set over the saucepan a stainless steel bowl, making sure the bottom of the bowl does not touch the water below. Add the chopped chocolate to the bowl and stir until it melts. Keep warm while you make the rest of the batter.

In a small saucepan over medium heat, melt the butter and continue cooking until it turns golden brown, about 8–10 minutes. Set aside.

In the bowl of a food processor or blender, combine the pasilla and ancho chiles, sugar, canela, cloves, and pumpkin seeds, and process into a fine powder. In the bowl of a standing mixer fitted with a whisk, or using a handheld blender and a large mixing bowl, beat together on low speed the eggs and vanilla. Add the chile mixture and beat on low for 10 more minutes. Add the melted chocolate, beat to incorporate, then add the butter, pouring in a slow, thin stream.

Pour the batter into 8 lightly oiled 4-ounce ramekins or cups. Place the cups in a large baking pan and put the baking pan on the oven rack. Pour hot water from a pitcher into the baking pan until the water reaches about halfway up the sides of the ramekins.

Bake for 13–14 minutes, remove from the oven, and allow to cool 10 minutes. Serve warm.

SOURCES

WWW.MELISSAGUERRA.COM A great selection of dried chiles, chocolates, herbs, spices, and more.

WWW.MEXGROCER.COM Ingredients, tortilla presses, comals, and packaged Mexican grocery items, such as mole pastes, spice rubs, and mixes.

WWW.LOSCHILEROS.COM A New Mexico–based company that sells dried chiles, blue corn, Mexican chocolate, and other items.

WWW.GOURMETSLEUTH.COM A wide range of Mexican ingredients, plus helpful information about most of them. They also sell wood chips for smoking.

WWW.HERBSOFMEXICO.COM A huge selection of herbs and teas.

WWW.PENZEYS.COM Spices, spices, and more spices. Plus some chiles.

WWW.ADRIANASCARAVAN.COM An excellent source for hard-to-find chiles and other ingredients.

WWW.COCINAMESTIZA.COM Good mole pastes from Mexico.

INDEX